This book belongs to:

Managing Editor
Mara Ellen Guckian

Editor in Chief
Brent L. Fox, M. Ed.

Creative Director
Sarah M. Fournier

Cover Artist
Kelly McMahon

Art Coordinator
Renée Mc Elwee

Illustrator
Kelly McMahon

Imaging
Amanda R. Harter

Publisher
Mary D. Smith, M.S. Ed.

Edupress
A Division of Teacher Created Resources, Inc.

12621 Western Avenue
Garden Grove, CA 92841
www.teachercreated.com

ISBN: 978-1-4206-0166-4
Reprinted, 2022

Made in U.S.A.

Edupress™
A Division of Teacher Created Resources

Introduction

This is a book to help young learners recognize and write the numbers zero through 10.

How to Use Page 3

This page offers an overview of the numbers being explored in this book. Each number is presented in bubble-form for young learners to color in. Next to each number is the correct number of circles that can also be filled in. These circles are provided to give young learners an example of "how many" each number represents.

Once colored, encourage your child to trace the bubble numbers with their fingers and touch and count each circle to reinforce each number amount. Point out the curves and straight lines used to form each number.

How to Use Pages 4–25

Practice pages are provided in this section to help develop a deeper understanding of numbers 0–10. Each number is presented on a 2-page spread:

- On the first page, young learners are guided to trace each number correctly and then practice writing the number on their own.
- On the second page of each spread, children are asked to find the featured number on the number line and then color the appropriate number of items. Both these skills will help develop *number sense*—the ability to understand numbers and number quantities. Encourage young learners to compare numbers and number amounts.

How to Use Pages 26–32

These pages provide additional practice recognizing numbers and number amounts. The final page is a traditional 100s chart.

Numbers 0–10

Color the numbers. Fill in the dots for each number.

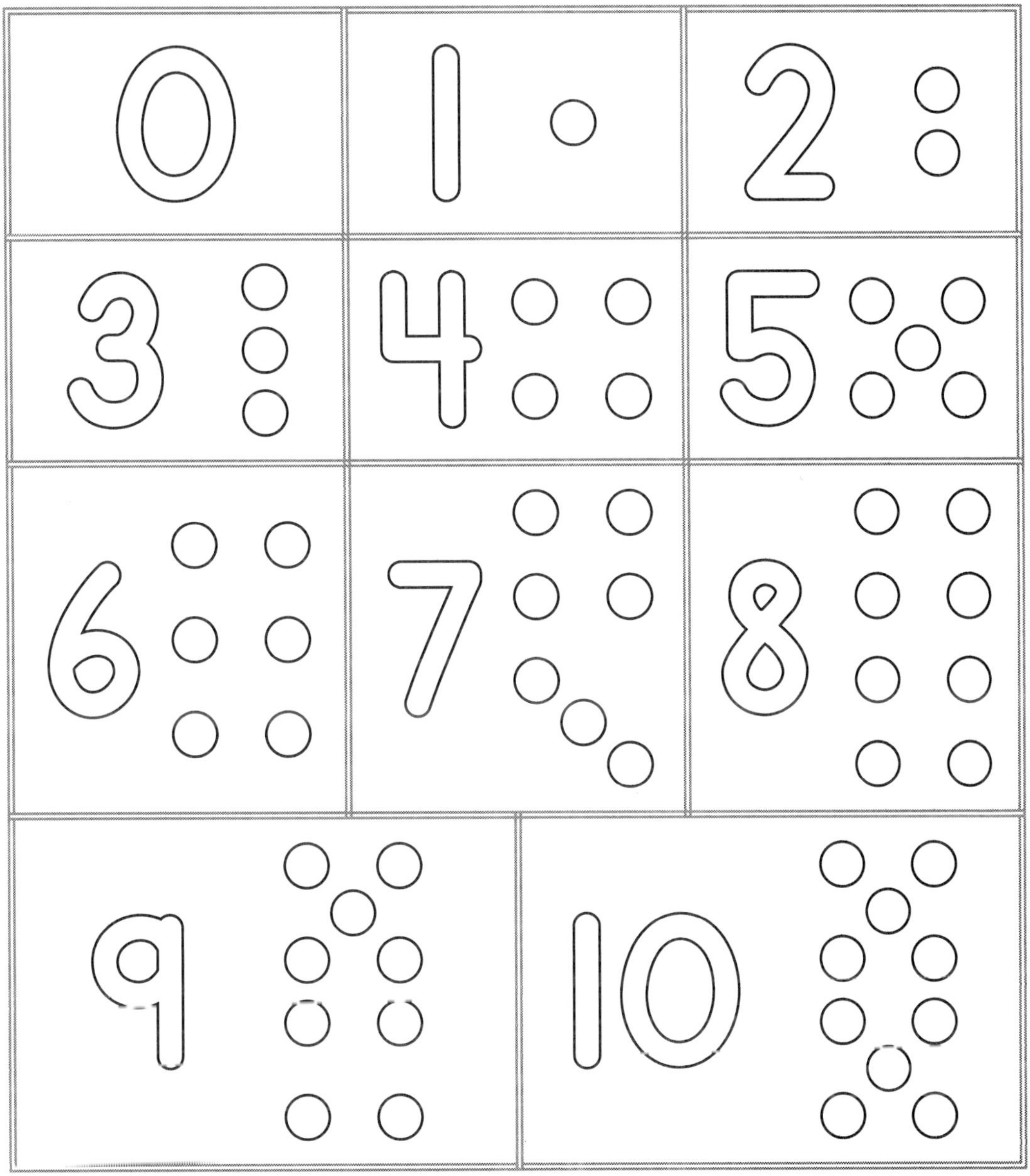

Zero 0

Trace the number **0**.

0 0 0 0 0

0 0 0 0 0

Write the number **0**.

Zero 0

Circle the number 0 on the number line.

Circle and color the box that has 0 cars.

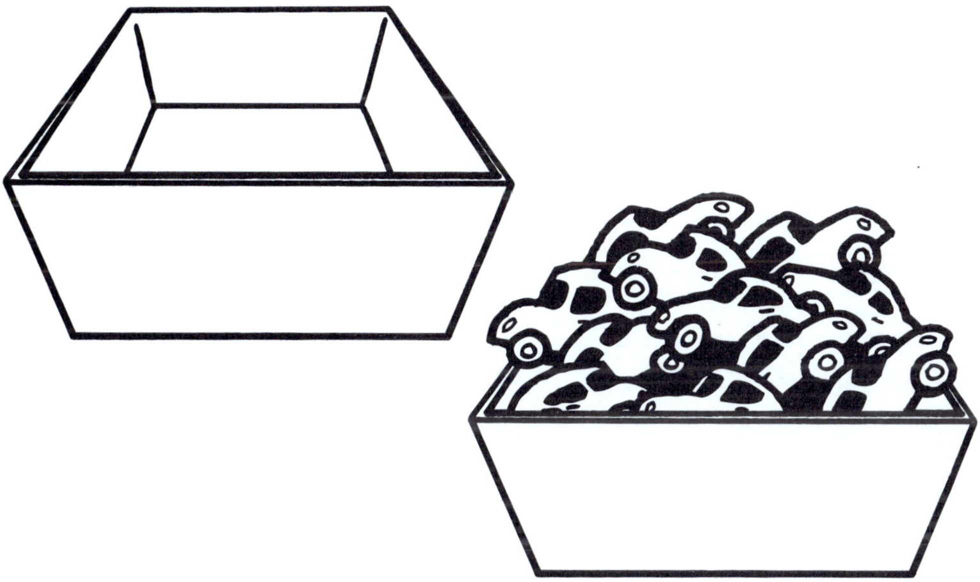

Trace and write the number word.

zero

One • 1

Trace the number 1.

Write the number 1.

One ● 1

Circle the number 1 on the number line.

0 1 2 3 4 5 6 7 8 9 10

There is 1 bird. Color it.

Trace and write the number word.

one

Two ●● 2

Trace the number **2.**

2 2 2 2 2

2 2 2 2 2

Write the number **2.**

Two ●● 2

Circle the number **2** on the number line.

0 1 2 3 4 5 6 7 8 9 10

Count and color the **2** dogs.

Trace and write the number word.

two

Three ●●● 3

Trace the number **3**.

3 3 3 3 3

3 3 3 3 3

Write the number **3**.

Three ●●● 3

Circle the number **3** on the number line.

0 1 2 3 4 5 6 7 8 9 10

Count and color the **3** fish.

Trace and write the number word.

three

Four ●●●● 4

Trace the number **4.**

4 4 4 4 4

4 4 4 4 4

Write the number **4.**

Four ●●●● 4

Circle the number **4** on the number line.

0 1 2 3 4 5 6 7 8 9 10

Count and color the **4** mice.

Trace and write the number word.

four

Five ●●●●● 5

Trace the number **5.**

5 5 5 5 5

5 5 5 5 5

Write the number **5.**

Five ●●●●● 5

Circle the number **5** on the number line.

0 1 2 3 4 5 6 7 8 9 10

Count and color the **5** monkeys.

Trace and write the number word.

five

Six ●●●●●● 6

Trace the number **6.**

6 6 6 6 6

6 6 6 6 6

Write the number **6.**

Six ●●●●●● 6

Circle the number **6** on the number line.

0 1 2 3 4 5 6 7 8 9 10

Count and color the **6** hens.

Trace and write the number word.

six

Seven ●●●●●●● 7

Trace the number **7.**

7 7 7 7 7

7 7 7 7 7

Write the number **7.**

Seven ●●●●●●● 7

Circle the number **7** on the number line.

0 1 2 3 4 5 6 7 8 9 10

Count and color the **7** rabbits.

Trace and write the number word.

seven

Eight ●●●●●●●● 8

Trace the number **8.**

8 8 8 8 8

8 8 8 8 8

Write the number **8.**

Eight ●●●●●●●● 8

Circle the number **8** on the number line.

0 1 2 3 4 5 6 7 8 9 10

Count and color the **8** sea stars.

Trace and write the number word.

eight

Nine ●●●●●●●●● 9

Trace the number **9.**

9 9 9 9 9

9 9 9 9 9

Write the number **9.**

Nine ●●●●●●●●● 9

Circle the number **9** on the number line.

0 1 2 3 4 5 6 7 8 9 10

Count and color the **9** flowers.

Trace and write the number word.

nine

Ten ●●●●●●●●●● 10

Trace the number **10.**

10 10 10 10

10 10 10 10

Write the number **10.**

Ten ●●●●●●●●●● 10

Circle the number **10** on the number line.

0 1 2 3 4 5 6 7 8 9 10

Count and color the **10** cupcakes.

Trace and write the number word.

ten

Count the Fish!

Draw lines from each number to the tank with the same number of fish.

3

4

5

6

Count the Fish!

Draw lines from each number to the tank with the same number of fish.

7

8

9

10

Ten Frames 1–5

Use the animal cards to help you color in the correct number of circles for each ten frame.

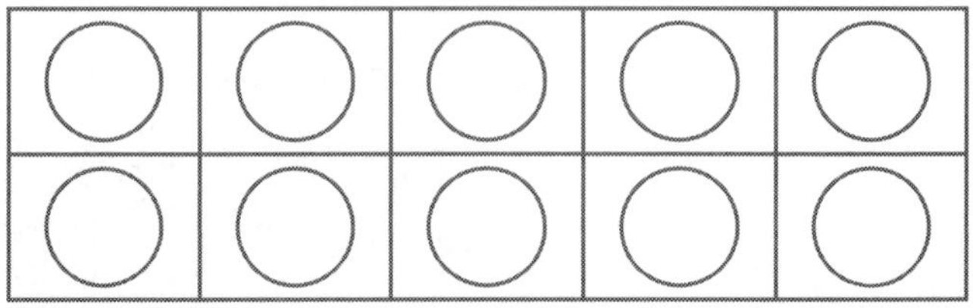

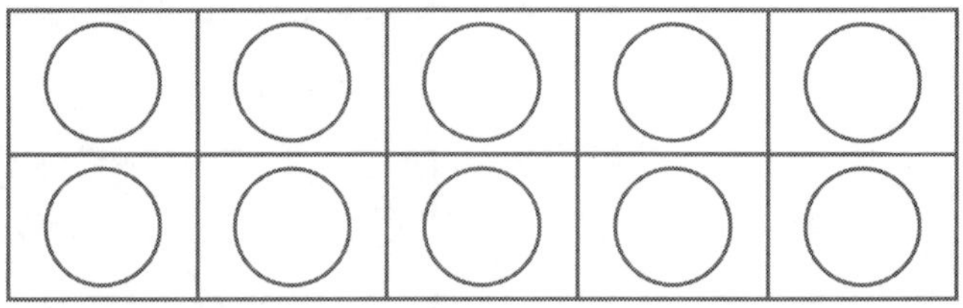

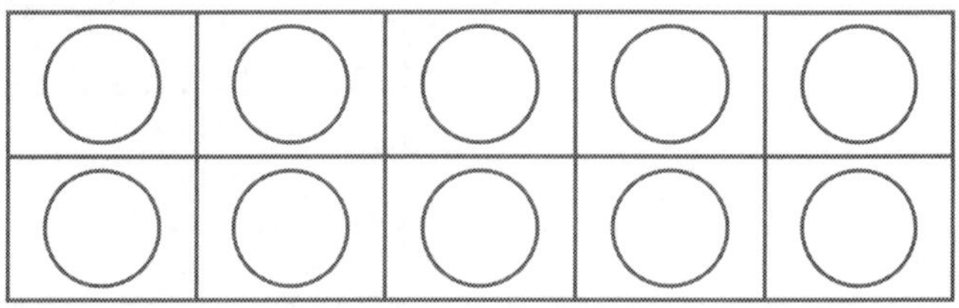

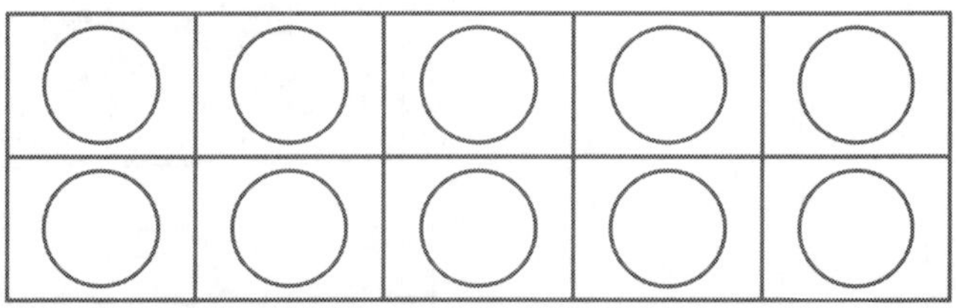

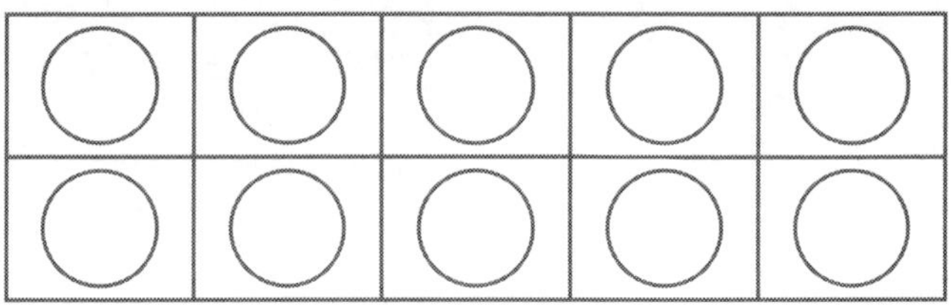

Ten Frames 6–10

Use the animal cards to help you color in the correct number of circles for each ten frame.

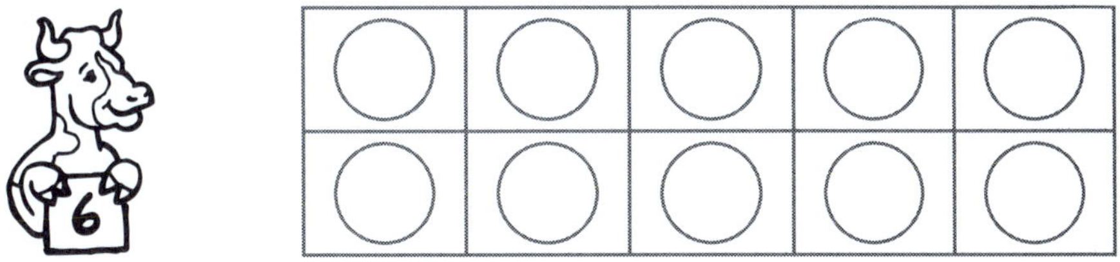

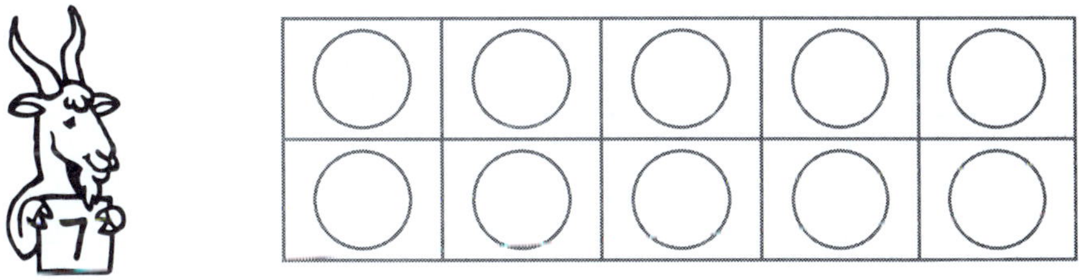

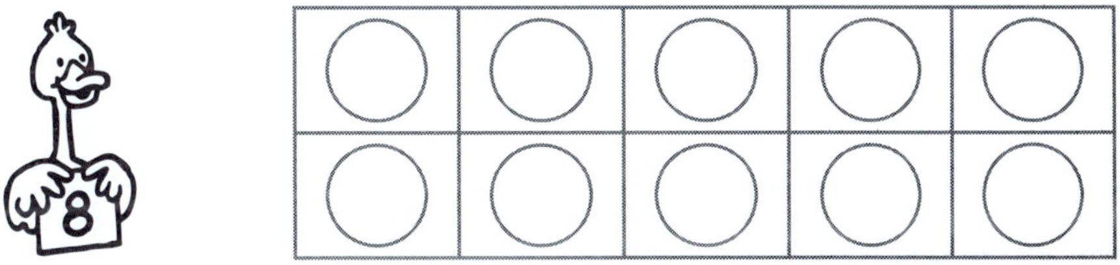

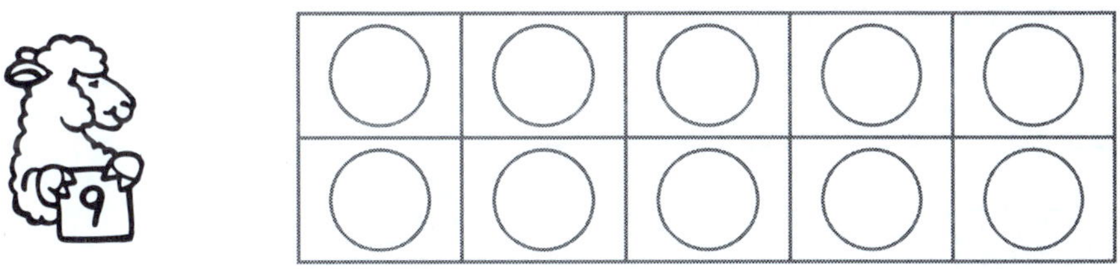

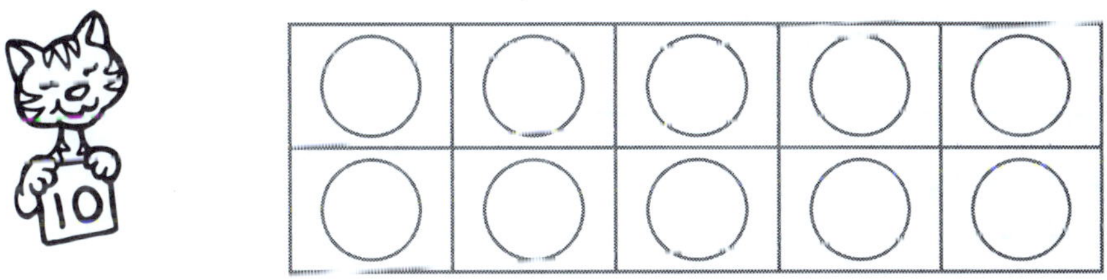

Number Words 0–5

Trace each number word and write its number next to it. Count the dots on each caterpillar.

zero 

one 

two 

three 

four 

five 

Number Words 6–10

Trace each number word and write its number next to it. Count the dots on each caterpillar.

six

seven

eight

nine

ten

What Comes After 10?

1	2	3	4	5	6	7	8	9	10
11	12	13	14	15	16	17	18	19	20
21	22	23	24	25	26	27	28	29	30
31	32	33	34	35	36	37	38	39	40
41	42	43	44	45	46	47	48	49	50
51	52	53	54	55	56	57	58	59	60
61	62	63	64	65	66	67	68	69	70
71	72	73	74	75	76	77	78	79	80
81	82	83	84	85	86	87	88	89	90
91	92	93	94	95	96	97	98	99	100

